READ ALL ABOUT IT!

Read All About

DANCE

by Christy Mitchinson

PEBBLE
a capstone imprint

Published by Pebble, an imprint of Capstone
1710 Roe Crest Drive, North Mankato, Minnesota 56003
capstonepub.com

Library of Congress Cataloging-in-Publication Data
Names: Mitchinson, Christy, author.
Title: Read all about dance / by Christy Mitchinson.
Description: North Mankato, Minnesota : Pebble, an imprint of Capstone, [2023] | Series: Read all about it | Includes index. | Audience: Ages 5-8 | Audience: Grades K-1 | Summary: "There is a dance style for everyone! Ballerinas sometimes dance on tiptoe. Tap dancers wear special shoes that make tapping sounds as they move. Some dancers make up their own moves while others follow a routine. Find out all about dance styles, equipment, studios, and more in this fact-filled book. Stunning photos give readers an up-close look at all kinds of dance, from hip-hop to Brazilian samba"— Provided by publisher.
Identifiers: LCCN 2022024837 (print) | LCCN 2022024838 (ebook) | ISBN 9780756572594 (hardcover) | ISBN 9780756573393 (paperback) | ISBN 9780756572563 (pdf) | ISBN 9780756572587 (kindle edition)
Subjects: LCSH: Dance—Juvenile literature.
Classification: LCC GV1596.5 .M58 2023 (print) | LCC GV1596.5 (ebook) | DDC 792.8—dc23
LC record available at https://lccn.loc.gov/2022024837
LC ebook record available at https://lccn.loc.gov/2022024838

Image Credits
Getty Images: adamkaz, top, 17, ARIS MESSINIS/AFP, bottom, 9, Bothwell Parirenyatwa / EyeEm, 9, Derek Hudson, top, 15, Eric McCandless, top, 19, Fiona Goodall, 12, Hauke-Christian Dittrich, bottom, 23, LIONEL BONAVENTURE, bottom, 19, Silver Screen Collection, bottom, 7, Stanton j Stephens, top, 23, Troy Aossey, Cover; Shutterstock: middle, 25, AePatt Journey, middle, 21, Africa Studio, top, 27, bottom, 30, amelipulen, 9, Anna55555, middle, 13, antoniodiaz, middle, 22, 29, BearFotos, Cover, middle, 25, Billion Photos, middle, 11, ChameleonsEye, top, 10, clicksdemexico, bottom, 27, Dana Balaz, 16, djile, bottom, 11, Elena11, top, 14, Everett Collection, bottom, 10, Everyonephoto Studio, top, 5, GAS-photo, 8, Hannamariah, bottom, 15, Ihor Bulyhin, middle, 24, Image Craft, top, 21, Karramba Production, bottom, 24, KBYC photography, bottom, 26, Kiselev Andrey Valerevich, top, 6, middle, 17, Korolevnina, top, 13, LightField Studios, 20, Maria Moroz, bottom, 5, Master1305, 4, top, 7, Max4e Photo, top, 11, middle, 15, Monica Macias, top, 26, Nataly Zavyalova, top, 25, New Africa, top, 30, Pavel L Photo and Video, bottom, 17, PeopleImages.com - Yuri A, bottom, 14, planet5D LLC, 28, RobertArt, top, 18, Roberto Galan, middle, 19, SFROLOV, middle, 6, Shamleen, bottom, 13, thunder50, middle, 18, VanessaRenee, bottom, 25, Vereshchagin Dmitry, top, 22

Editorial Credits
Editor: Carrie Sheely; Designer: Bobbie Nuytten; Media Researcher: Donna Metcalf; Production Specialist: Tori Abraham

Table of Contents

Words in **bold** are in the glossary.

Chapter 1

What Is Dance?

Dance is moving your body in time with music. There are lots of ways to dance. Some people take dance classes to learn. But you don't have to take classes to be able to dance!

There are two main ways to dance: freestyle or following a routine.

Freestyle means dancing any way you want to the music.

Following a routine means dancing to moves that have been planned for that music.

Freestyle dancers use the music and how it makes them feel to choose how to move.

5

Freestyle moves are common in hip-hop dance, a style often performed to **rap** music.

Dance teachers can create their own routines for their students or hire a **choreographer**.

In 2017, Odumewu Debbie set a Guiness World Record for the longest dancing **marathon** by one person. She danced freestyle for 137 hours!

Freestyle dance can include runs, kicks, spins, jumps, turns, and leaps.

Famous choreographer Bob Fosse won eight Tony Awards. Dancers perform his style around the world.

Chapter 2

History of Dance

Dancing has been around a lot longer than you might think. There is proof that people were dancing in ancient times.

The oldest pictures of dancing were found in cave paintings in India from around 8000 BCE. That means people were dancing more than 10,000 years ago!

In ancient Egypt, people used music and dance to honor their religion and as a way to tell stories.

For hundreds of years, dance has been an important part of African **culture**.

Dance routines during **ceremonies** have been part of the Olympic Games since ancient times.

The lion dance began more than 1,000 years ago. It is often performed at events in China.

In the 1500s and 1600s, ballet became an important part of the lives of the rich during the Renaissance period in Italy.

The waltz is the oldest ballroom dance. It dates back to the 1600s in Austria.

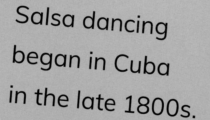

Salsa dancing began in Cuba in the late 1800s.

As new styles of music are made, new styles of dance are also created.

Chapter 3

Dance Around the World

People around the world dance for many different reasons. Some dance as part of a **tradition** or to show pride in where they live. Some dance just to have fun.

To do haka from New Zealand, dancers stomp their feet, clap their hands, and shout.

Bollywood dance is a style often seen in movies from India.

Spanish Flamenco dancers snap their fingers and clap their hands to guitar music.

Dragon dancers in China use poles to hold a dragon made of fabric and bamboo.

Kabuki is an old Japanese dance style that includes acting and singing.

Samba dancers perform in costumes at the famous Carnival of Brazil.

The Adumu in Africa is a competitive jumping dance where boy dancers form a circle and take turns jumping as high as they can.

The Viennese waltz from Austria has constant turns to the left and right.

In the Irish step dance, dancers move their feet quickly but keep their upper bodies stiff.

Chapter 4

Popular Dance Styles

The styles that are most popular depend on where you live. But some styles are taught almost everywhere.

In ballet, ballerinas dance to **classical** music, sometimes on tiptoe.

Tap dancers tap to the music with their feet wearing special shoes.

Modern dancers use their movements to show how the music makes them feel.

In step dance, people use their feet to make sounds.

17

Competition is at the heart of hip-hop dance. Dancers compete with each other in "battles."

Ballroom dance includes partner dances such as waltz, polka, and swing.

TV shows and movies about dancing have helped increase the popularity of dance.

Pom dance is a type of dance popular in American high schools where dancers use handheld pom-poms.

The Paris Opera Ballet School is one of the world's most famous ballet companies.

Chapter 5

Dance Studios

Dance studios are where people go to learn to dance by taking classes. Studios may have classes for only one style or several styles.

As of 2020, there were more than 54,000 dance studios in the United States.

Some studios have one big room. Others have lots of smaller rooms.

Studio floors can be wooden or matted. Mats protect dancers' bodies if they do moves such as flips.

Large studios may have a theater to hold performances.

A studio has a mirrored wall so dancers can see their moves.

A **barre** is mounted to a wall for dancers to stretch and do exercises.

Dancers need music, so each studio has a sound system or a piano.

Studios from around the world compete in international competitions.

Chapter 6

Dance Clothing and Shoes

Dancers wear different dance clothes and shoes for each style. For some styles, dancers wear no shoes at all! The soles of dance shoes are usually covered in suede. This soft material makes it easier to turn on the dance floor.

Ballet dancers wear **leotards** and soft ballet slippers.

Experienced ballerinas wear **pointe shoes** to dance on the tips of their toes.

Jazz shoes are similar to ballet slippers except they usually lace up and are often black.

Most of the time, modern dancers dance barefoot.

Country line dancers dress in Western hats and clothing.

Flamenco dancers wear sturdy shoes with heels.

Hip-hop dancers often wear tennis shoes and casual clothing, including baggy pants and T-shirts.

Tap gets its name from the tapping sounds made by metal plates attached to tap shoes.

Women who do ballroom dance often dance in 2-inch- (5-centimeter-) high heels. Latin dancers' heels can be as high as 3 inches (7.6 cm)!

Folk dancers often wear traditional costumes based on where they live.

Chapter 7

Learning to Dance

Do you want to learn to dance? There are many ways to prepare and get started!

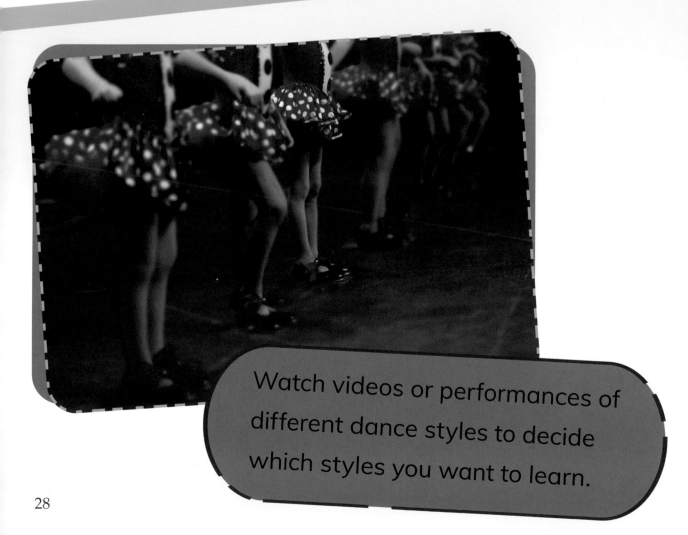

Watch videos or performances of different dance styles to decide which styles you want to learn.

Ask your friends to teach you dances they know.

Check to see if there are any dance classes or clubs in your area available to join.

Follow along with the steps or routines in how-to videos online.

Remember to do stretching and warm-up exercises before you dance and cool-down exercises afterward.

Glossary

barre—a handrail to support dancers as they stretch and perform exercises

ceremony—a formal event to celebrate or mark a special occasion

choreographer—a person, usually a trained dancer, who makes up, or choreographs, dances for classes and performances

classical—a type of music that is often from the 1700s or 1800s and is played by musicians without singers

culture—a people's way of life, ideas, art, customs, and traditions

leotard—a stretchy one-piece outfit that dancers wear to train and perform

marathon—an event that tests how long someone can do something

pointe shoes—ballet shoes with a hard box in the toe to allow ballerinas to dance on the tips of their toes

rap—a type of music of African American origin in which rhythmic and usually rhyming speech is chanted to music

tradition—a custom, idea, or belief passed down through time

Index

About the Author

Christy Mitchinson is a writer, all-star cheerleading coach, and wild bird rehabber. When she isn't writing, reading, or coaching, she works with ill and injured wild magpies, crows, and more to get them well and ready to go back into the wild. She lives in Warrington, United Kingdom, with her husband, two kids, and a mini zoo.